Dreaminations

Prose Poems

Dreaminations

Prose Poems

Jianqing Zheng

MADVILLE
PUBLISHING

LAKE DALLAS, TEXAS

Requests for permission to reprint or reuse material
from this work should be sent to:

Permissions
Madville Publishing
PO Box 358
Lake Dallas, TX 75065

Cover Photo: Jianqing Zheng
Cover Design: Kim Davis

ISBN: 978-1-963695-49-6 paperback
978-1-936695-50-2 ebook
Library of Congress Control Number: 2025945610

*In memory of Theodore Haddin (1933–2024),
friend and fellow poet*

Contents

III

I

Looking Out the Window

There was a sky-high pine tree in the backyard years ago. It functioned like a bagpipe of autumn wind to blow "Amazing Grace" or an overlook tower for clouds to linger and see the chasing squirrels. Yet, it died after years of persistence to stand on our guard. One night a lightning bolt hit the tree and burned a vertical strip that ran down the trunk to the ground.

Its glory started to fade, and its bottom was hollowed into an animal den. Its needles browned and dropped one after another. The bare top looked like a bald head. Its cones thudded on the shed roof like the sudden loud beats of a metal drum. After its bark peeled like old rags, its limbs looked like the white bones of a skeleton shimmering in the moonlight, foreboding a slow death. Crows frequented it in twos and threes, crying a mourning song.

Sometimes a redheaded woodpecker paid a visit, knocking branch to branch but doing nothing useful. We decided to bring it down in case tornadoes blew it over to crush our house or our neighbor's. One October day, a chainsaw amputated it. Piece by piece, it thumped on the ground, like a farewell blues.

autumn dawn
a reishi mushroom
by the stump

Moonplay

Tired of sitting on the deck watching the new moon bobbing in the dark pond and hearing frogs croaking against the quiet night, the man plops into water to startle the moon into a fluttering bird, but it rocks away like an origami boat. Then he flails the water, intending to turn it over; it slithers away like a silverfish. After moonplay, the man rolls over to backstroke and floats like a log on the moonlit ripples sparkling in fish scales. Now the moon shines like a paper lantern in a weeping willow; the man dogpaddles to shore.

    rippling moonlight
    a kajika frog's croak
    louder and louder

Touch

At dusk, a boy with a jar in his hand runs to the stream to catch fireflies while his dad walks to a dock to take a picture of a rowboat turning itself with the flow. After the snapshot, the man sees a firefly glowing on and off before him. He flings his hand to catch it and calls out to his son, but the boy is enjoying himself. He moves his hands up and down to touch the glowing bugs while his jar is bobbing away down the stream. Seeing this, the man releases his catch. When he was his son's age, he stood in the shallows to have a pleasant touch of the fireflies. Now sunset dims out behind weeping willows, and his son dims into a silhouette surrounded by fireflies sparkling like stars.

> July 4—
> a constellation
> of fireworks

Then and Now

Swallows once skating on the rink of the morning sky chirp only in the warm wind of dreams. Gray smog, heavy and thick, spreads in the sky to shroud the city into a dying place. When night falls, people in the street look like walking apparitions, the moon a pale skull.

> sudden gale
> dust swept up
> across the fields
> the sun a scarecrow
> blown away

Killing Time

Staying home with nothing to do on New Year's Day, I turn on the computer to view the pictures taken a year ago in a southern ghost town by the Mississippi River. A church window catches my attention. Wondering why I took this picture in the abandoned church, I converted the image into a black and white negative: the window looks like an upright black coffin, and the bare whitish vines in it like a standing ghost coming from history.

> power off
> the old couple
> stargaze

Just Wondering

When bits of green on a young pecan tree burst into tender leaves, they attract a tail-wagging squirrel to nibble. Often a mockingbird appears. It swoops, squabbles, and pesters, scaring the little brown sprinter to skitter from sprig to sprig and scurry out of sight. The bird then lands on the treetop and chants. A courting, a territorial song, a parody?

    whispering wind
    sprays of white spirea
    nod by the fence

A Way of Watching

Recuperating from a broken leg after falling off the ladder, I spend plenty of time sitting by the window watching birds. They sing intermittently on the tallow tree—a warbler's chirp, a blue jay's squawk, a mockingbird's tongue-twister, a mourning dove's coo. Their songs hearten me to whistle at them delightfully in the face of my inability to walk. The most joyful view is a loud cheer each morning: a cardinal shining bright red among fresh green.

> moon leaps
> onto the porch swing
> to curl up
> a low jangle
> in the empty evening

After Storm

Sam leans the ladder against the gutter and climbs to the roof to remove the twigs broken off the dying oak by the night thunderstorm. Shaking like a scarecrow in the wind, he cautiously pulls the big twigs to the edge, pushes them to the ground, sweeps the small ones, patches the punched holes, and replaces the damaged shingles. Then he climbs down like a slow koala. Feeling an ice pack on his back, he goes mowing. In one hard pull, the mower roars, a charging bull Sam pushes as if treading in mud. An hour later, sweat wet through his shirt makes him feel better, but the cloudy sky looks pale, a patient with a sudden loss of blood flow.

    empty day
    hanami
    on tv

River

Rivers are lifelines of all things; river plains are cradles of ancient civilizations. Whether long or short, a river has its characteristics, form, history, waterway, and geography that integrate culture, agriculture, migration, habitation, art, folktale, and hydrology. It flows into a sea, a lake, or another river. Without a flowing body of water, there is no existence of life. Such is the greatness of water that forms us, irrigates our bodies, nurtures our souls.

A river or a lake articulates itself and urges us to ponder our inseparable connection with it. It is a compound of life, love, and necessity. In the meandering flow of memories, a river, a stream, a lake, or a pond connects its water and its people. It can be Wordsworthian to stand on a bridge to have an overflow of feelings; it can be Thoreauvian to pace in deep thought around a pond; it can be simply a physical and spiritual pleasure to step into a stream to flyfish, to camp by a mountain creek, or to sing and dance in the rain like Gene Kelly.

> floating in the river
> of memories
> a houseboat

River has also been a metaphor for the passing of time. Heraclitus, an ancient Greek philosopher, professed, "You can't step twice into the same river." Confucius, an ancient Chinese philosopher, sighed by a river, "Things that flow on like this never stop day or night." Life continues over time like a river flowing in the past, present, future, and infinity.

Whatever impressions a river or a body of water leaves on you must have a special watermark in your heart. In a sense, both water and you interconnect. Numerous luminaries have described this connection. William Butler Yeats yearned to return to Innisfree when lake water was lapping "in the deep heart's core;" T. S. Eliot beheld the co-existence of individuality and eternity in "The river is within us, the sea is all about us;" Langston Hughes released his emotions by saying he had known "rivers ancient as the world and older than the flow of human blood in human veins;" and Charley Patton, king of the Delta blues, sang about the disaster of the Great Mississippi Flood of 1927 that threatened the life of African Americans in "High Water Everywhere."

> river sunset
> fire and water crackle
> into stars

To me, living in the Mississippi Delta for three decades, the river is the silent rhythm of daily life or the stomping backbeat of memories. I am a river lover because I was born and grew up by the Long River in China. I swam in it, caught shrimp from it, wrote poems about it. Many evenings, I walked five minutes to the riverside to jog or enjoy a moment of being by the river. Now I live an hour away from the Mississippi, another long river. I feel the two rivers flow in me. Their confluence makes me associate one in my eyes with the other in my memory. Sometimes I drive to the levee or a river park for a meeting with the Mississippi River. The river parks in Helena, Arkansas, and in Tunica, Mississippi, are my favorite places to go, where I like to sit on a pier bench or in a porch rocking chair to enjoy a momentary stay with the Big Muddy or close my eyes to let the river breeze massage my mind. When the riverscape becomes the mindscape, it flows in the veins, laps with the heartbeat, leaves its watermarks in the poems.

We need the river to live; we need the river to enrich our spiritual life and inspire our creative writing as well. Step twice into the river for tranquility and confluence and let it flow past us, within us, be us!

> river wind
> ripples into
> an amazing maze

Goodbye

Goodbye may mean departure, detachment, death, divorce, breakup, change for a new life, promising career, or bright future. There are different ways to say goodbye, such as farewell, adieu, bon voyage, or zaijian. Sometimes the word carries nuances of meaning. The opposite of the word is badbye or sadbye, so bye can be awful, beautiful, fearful, joyful, mournful, mirthful, painful, peaceful, sorrowful, tearful, or wistful.

The Chinese Tang Dynasty poet Li Po used imagery in a quatrain to express his goodbye about seeing off Meng Haoran, an elder friend he admired:

> After departing the Yellow Crane Tower, my old friend
> sails downriver to Yangzhou when catkins fuzz March.
> His lonely boat disappears beyond the blue horizon,
> and in sight now is the Long River flowing skyward.

I didn't feel sad when I departed the village where I was sent for reeducation during the Chinese Cultural Revolution. It was a cold morning that even roosters wouldn't crow and dogs wouldn't bark. The village was sleeping, and the rain fell on my umbrella like crying tears. The dirt road soaked by rain became soft and muddy. Each step forward was like lifting heavy weights, but I trod on with a light heart, knowing I was leaving for good. I still remember the last image of the village:

> looking back
> my muddy footprints
> run toward me

Where Are You From?

There are different answers because the question can be geographical, political, racial, and ethnic; it can also mean curiosity, attitude, suspicion, or exclusion. I'm from a city in central China, where twelve million people bump like dumplings in a big wok. It's divided by two rivers, the Yangtze (the Long River), the third longest in the world, and the Han River, the longest tributary of the Long River. I lived there for thirty-some years before migrating to Mississippi, where I have lived for another thirty-some years. Interestingly, life has been divided into two halves like two half-brothers. The first half has faded like ink on old manuscripts, but the second still acts like a naughty boy wading with pants rolled up.

> September 4
> a call to renew
> *Native Son*

Geographically, everyone has an origin and knows where they are from. Yet, the question of "where are you from?" can branch out into different ones if we think beyond the box, the self, the race, or the country: Are we from Earth or elsewhere? Are we distant brothers or sisters who are now in different colors? Are our forebears from Africa or another planet in the universe? Who created us or who brought us to Earth? Is Earth hell or paradise? All this comes to one basic question: Where are you from?

> prayer time
> eyes closed
> on second coming

We are used to living in the confines of our own races, cultures, and boundaries. We think good fences make good friends, yet the sad reality is that we are separated by colors, railroads, rivers, or invisible whatnots such as classes, likes, dislikes, or circles. Location is not just a common mantra for realty sales. It indicates value, safety, "rich" or "poor" area, separation, or what's been given attention or ignored intentionally, economically, politically, and racially. Sometimes we refuse to see and think or approach others who are not part of us; sometimes we even refuse to know ourselves and our surroundings or are denied belonging to a community, a workplace, or a country. We may not know about the Fourteenth Amendment to the Constitution, the Chinese Exclusion Act, and the internment of Japanese Americans in World War II, all of which revert to the question of where you are from.

> night wind
> a blues song whines into
> cottonfields

A Retired Man's World

Sinking into the porch sofa, he kills time imagining varied forms of a large yard rock enlivened by the shift of light and shade: a reclining laughing Buddha holding a golden ingot in hand, an old monk reciting sutra under a Bodhi tree, a Sphinx with a blank stare, a Sisyphus gasping from pushing a boulder up the hill. When his wife steps out and pats him on the shoulder for lunch, he chimes to her as if in a beautiful dream that the rock looks like Rodin's sculpture of hugging lovers, and she teases that it's him, an old snoring Durin. The old man mumbles no, then says it's a magnet that absorbs thunder's grumble, wind's whistle, rain's pitapat, or a hard chunk from Skull Hill. And his wife giggles, joking it's an overlook for him to see the world. Yet, it's not always his overlook. Sometimes a mockingbird lands on it to sing like Taylor Swift. On a lazy afternoon, a skinny cat scoots across the street to squat by it, waiting to catch a leaping squirrel.

> snoopy sun
> an old dog squints
> at a passerby

Missing

Mom cooks alone while others chat in the den or watch Macy's Thanksgiving Day Parade. Now and then, Dad gets up from his reclining chair and wobbles to the kitchen to help. But Mom doesn't need an extra hand on her backstage. When she places dinner on the table and after Dad says grace, we become hungry performers on the front stage. Forks and knives start tap dancing while Mom laughs like tinkling wind chimes.

    ginkgo leaves
    the churchyard covered
    with golden sunshine

Memory of Mom's Cat

When the sunset straddles atop the cabin like a red-faced cowboy on a bronco, Tigger scoots in through the cat door, a squirrel clamped between his jaws. He saunters to the den to show the prey to Mom who's watching *The Golden Girls*. "How dare you!" Mom pats her hand on the couch arm. Stunned, Tigger bolts out. In a while, he returns and crouches on the kitchen floor to sniff at his dinner plate. After one lick, he wanders to the den and rubs his arched back against Mom's shanks. When she claps her hands, Tigger leaps onto her lap for a stroke.

Christmas gift
an embroidered cat
for Mom

Curious

The neighbor's tuxedo cat prowls in the lilyturfs with spikes of tiny bluebells by the weathered picket fence of my side yard. He lowers his head, twitches his ears, and snatches his right paw. In a second, a small snake struggles between his jaws. Tuxedo swaggers away, tail wagging. Soon a beige cat comes to search the same spot but leaves empty-pawed. Watching from my study window, I wonder how the two feline creatures communicate about the catch. Through meows or an olfactory language?

> some ants circle
> a drop of Terro bait
> some go as messengers
> a pheromone line
> hurries out of a slab crack

Homework

Tom wants April to cut a tad bit off the sides after she wraps the red cape around him and fastens the straps behind his neck. "Ok." The hair clipper hums gladly like a lawnmower. Twenty minutes later, her masterpiece appears in the mirror. His crown looks like the front lawn he mowed. Frowning at the light stubble, Tom sighs, "Cut too short. It's to be outgrown with weeds." His wife pats his head like a tambourine.

    pillow talk
    the kiss blooms into
    a kiss-me-not

II

A Delta Weekend

Wearing a broad smile, my wife steps into the kitchen. Breakfast is waiting on the table: a bowl of oatmeal with honey, walnut halves, red goji, and black sesame powder, as well as a dish of sliced pink lady. A cordial waiter with a sharp memory, I pull the chair for her.

> morning sun
> the orange tabby cat
> gives a burp

Half an hour later, I serve as her chauffeur, driving her to the mall in Memphis. I wait like a terracotta warrior outside the fitting room or doze in the shoe area with a big shopping bag resting on my knees. When the sun sneaks down, we are on our way back to Greenwood. My wife catnaps, and I yawn with eyes welling up with tears.

> fleeting clouds
> the moon's grin
> off and on

A Stay Against Confusion

Sipping a cup of oolong for relaxation, I stretch my legs and accidentally knock a stack of books off the tea table. I guess they need a break as well, so I let them lie listless on the floor, one's head on the other's chest, the other two leaning back to back with lowered heads, the rest like toppled dominoes, and the one I've paged the whole afternoon snoring gently.

    spiritless wind
    sunlight swings slightly
    with sheer curtains
    my Russian Blue
    twitches her tail

Not in Vain

After the Hemingway Museum, my wife and I stroll to Garbo's Grill to savor mango dogs. We stand chewing in the summer sun as a few roosters strut around like fashion models. Patting my stuffed belly, I suggest window-shopping along Duval. In an art gallery, a photograph of a snowy egret catches our eyes. It's titled "Calling." "Is it courting?" my wife whispers, as if the bird may startle and flap away. At the entrance of an antique shop, I bump into a life-size cardboard cutout of Robert Johnson, a smirk lifting the corner of his mouth. The bluesman stands there like a doorman, ready to welcome us in. One of Johnson's songs comes to mind. Changing the words, I sing like mumbling: "I walk with you to the hotel hand in hand." My wife waves her hand like driving off a buzzing fly, but I keep singing as we stroll to the hotel. "It's not hard at all to tell love is surely in vain..."

bodhi walk step by step into nothing

Transference

While I watch the winking greenish light of fireflies in the backyard, a couple of mosquitoes dance before my eyes. I raise my hand to wave them away. Ouch! A shocking pain pierces my upper arm. Weeks later, pain takes the other arm. Since both arms are like brittle branches unable to bend, I rub my back itch against the door frame like a bear scratching against a tree trunk. My wife suggests swaying my arms slowly to release the tension, but they move like wipers on broken pivot nuts. Day after day, stiffness builds up. I go to a pain specialist, who, after reviewing my CT scan, says he finds nothing abnormal. His head shakes like a pellet drum. Perhaps pain plays hide-and-seek.

    rising sun
    a redheaded
    woodpecker
    knocks around
    a dead branch

Quiet Departure

Diagnosed with advanced lung cancer, Uncle Tank knows he'll die soon. One Saturday afternoon he asks his wife Liz to drive him to Ocean Springs where they first met. As they wobble to the pier, seagulls on the railings burst into low air. Some land back or flap away, some drift overhead and shriek like squeaking hinges.

    deep autumn
    reeds along the shore
    wavy white

They sit on the bench, reminiscing about how they first met forty years ago. Their voices lap like wavelets while the sun sinks over the horizon. "It's time to go home," Tank murmurs, wanting to sleep well so he'll have some energy to rake leaves. He never wakes up. A layer of oak leaves, like Aunt Liz's memory, covers the yard.

    Christmas Eve
    reading
    old greeting cards

Attachment

homebound
a landscape calendar
on the backseat

Jon and Jane pace to the beach after attending Uncle Tank's funeral
in Ocean Springs. They sit on a pier bench to feel the massage of sea
wind. Jon recalls an old pier where Tank and his wife Liz liked to sit
on a bench chatting or listening to waves lap, but Hurricane Katrina
blew it away.

fall evening
empty the mind
to the sea

Raised by Tank and Liz after his parents died in a car crash, Jon has
a close relationship with his uncle and auntie. He says he enjoyed his
playtime as a little boy on Saturday afternoons, building sandcastles
with Liz or flyfishing on the pier with Tank.

story time
even stars perk up
their ears

A brown pelican hunches on a pillar as if in a trance. It leers when Jon
moves closer to grab a shot. "Don't disturb the bird." Jane's soft voice
sounds more and more like Liz's. On the beach, a playful boy runs
after seagulls.

memory
a fishing float bobbing
up and down

Old Field Road Sign, Mount Locust, Mississippi

The engraved sign shows a young woman with a basket in her hand walking down the road, her long skirt swaying like sunlight rustling with shriveled leaves. Is she taking lunch to her husband harvesting cotton or going berry picking in the woods?

> fall solitude
> Spanish moss hangs
> from live oaks

I follow her to the cemetery. A white marble obelisk, standing there like a historic landmark, reveals her name and dates of birth and death. She's been at rest since 1849. I take a snapshot of her and pace back to the parking lot. Footsteps echo the long past.

> empty dusk
> a split-rail fence
> zigzags

Sightseeing

The damp, slippery path by Windsor Ruins leads nowhere but to the bony, mud-brown vines that tangle in the bleak February wind. Like the remaining Corinthian columns, those vines twist and crawl to extend the intensity of life into a labyrinthine tale of the mansion once with southern glory.

blank sky
a crow's cry glides
over woods

A Stop in Port Gibson, Mississippi

A golden hand atop the steeple. Its index finger points upright at the sky, indicating the direction we are bound to go. Does it point to a place where souls unite, where husband and wife date again, where we speak one language, where there's no foul play of colors? I look up; the hand shines hard in morning sun.

> homebound
> passing a road called
> No Name Rd

In the Drunk's Eye

A beer can rolls in the middle of the blacktop and leaps up to tap dance like Fred Astaire. It slips, loses balance, tumbles to the curb, and lies there like a drunk. Soon it climbs up, staggers back to the road, and raps with backward rolls, pitch-tucks, front somersaults. After bowing, it wobbles away, eyes bulged like Homer Simpson's. Then it returns to perform drunken boxing: sway, hit, dodge, grapple, feint. Before it bounces away like a dancing piggy, an ambulance, sirens blaring, crushes it flat.

> midnight juke
> saxophone wails
> a rueful tune

In Another Country

A newcomer to the new world, Langlang's mama starts to learn English at thirty-five. One morning after preparing breakfast, she hollers in English, "Son, brakefast ready." No answer. The boy, who played games online last night, is still in bed. She brushes to his bedroom and whispers into his ear, "Brakefast ready."

"Brake fast? What's that?" Langlang mumbles.
"Break first!" her tone is emphatic and pitchy.
"What first?"
"Ea' first!"

Then she pinches his mouth gently, smirking, "Don' wha' wha' like a Chihuahua. Jum' out bed and ea' hot-sour noodles." After his mother walks back to the kitchen, Langlang rubs his eyes, grunting, "Hot-sour noodles? Never heard of it. I'll eat cereal."

He crawls out of bed and moves sleepily to the kitchen, like a clumsy turtle on sand. As soon as he sits at the table, Langlang breaks wind, as loud as the sudden popping of a running lawnmower. His mama frowns, "Mind your manners. Don' far' when you ea your breakfart!"

> Big Buddha temple
> all languages flow
> to the golden statue

The Existence of Time

We live in a constant flow of moments. Every second is formless in two sounds: tick and tock. Every Tao has two directions: backward and forward. Everything is a transient response: a yawn, a chirp, a raindrop, a bolt of lightning, a sneeze making the whole class say God bless you, a word forgotten instantly in the middle of thinking, a freight train clunking through the village.

> quiet morning
> two empty chairs
> on the porch
> a mockingbird
> leaps to and fro

A Sense of Place

My dear colleague Dr. Marla Cowie passed away on November 22, 2021. She retired twenty years ago and moved to the Gulf Coast, but after Hurricane Katrina destroyed her house, she relocated to Hot Springs, Arkansas. She told me once that she was from the Lake Michigan area and Hot Springs was an ideal place to live because it had mountains and lakes. Marla's words reveal an attachment to a place in the deep heart's core, showing her memory and nostalgia.

blue mist dream of the lake adrift

This attachment or sense of place fascinates writers. When Yeats walked down London's Fleet Street, a fountain in a shop window tinkling like a call to return intensified his homesickness for a murmur in "The Lake Isle of Innisfree": "I will arise and go now, for always night and day / I hear lake water lapping with low sounds…in the deep heart's core." This call to return struck Willie Morris too. To him, the sense of place is home, is Mississippi. In *My Mississippi*, Morris mentions that when his New York friends didn't understand why he had to return to Mississippi, he said, "Well, it's home…I've got to go." Richard Wright, another Mississippian, dreams of his sense of place in *Black Boy*: "There was the vague sense of the infinite as I looked down upon the yellow, dreaming waters of the Mississippi River from the verdant bluffs of Natchez."

homesick a float going up and down

In a sense, a place can strike sparks for us to see, imagine, write about. Poet Dick Lourie wrote me that quite a few of my poems had the water image. My homeplace is a metropolitan city divided into three parts by the Yangtze and the Han rivers. Now I live by the Mississippi River. To me, water connects places and memories on both sides of the Pacific.

net hauling red sunset flopping with fish

35

Road to Pig Out

While driving, I listen to the radio talk on biology research, which ends with a humorous twist. The female biologist answers, "No fungi!" when asked if that's her research, and the male host quickly turns her words into another question: "No fond guys?" Both burst out laughing. My wife dozing in shotgun nods and giggles.

BBQ ad:
Wednesday is Ladies Day
Buy One Get One Free

The River of God

I walk to the bridge to take pictures of the riverside trees crowned with the golden shine of sunset, but the reflection of the sky wavering into bluish ripples catches my eye. I move from one end of the bridge to the other to shoot the ripples from different angles while trees lose their splendid moment. They stand in line like silent disciples. So do I, stunned by the river flowing like the Holy Ghost's procession into bloody twilight.

> going home
> a sign blinks by a streetlight:
> In God We Trust

Dusk at a Southern Town

A car blasts loud rap and swaggers down the street of this southern town. It screeches to a sudden stop when a drunk ignoring its coming stumbles to the other side. The driver sticks his head out the window hollering with a cloud of thick weed smoke, but the jaywalker waddles away like a quacking duck stirred up by the noisy rap. He drags his feet into the package store where he will grab a twelve-pack of Blue Moon to dizzy the night. Behind him, the slanting sun smirks through the store's glass door guarded by security bars.

barren street
sunlight swept away
by autumn wind

III

Right of Way

Jim walks to his office after the meeting in the Criminal Justice department. His stomach growls like a baby's hunger whimper. As he microwaves the Healthy Choice beef teriyaki, he hears a knock. It's Precious from Student Counseling. Behind her are a student and her parents. She asks if Jim will allow Myoshi to take Organized Crime as an independent study because owing to a safety issue with her peers, Myoshi must go home. Jim agrees, and they all look relieved. After they leave, he wonders what independent study means if bullying persists on campus.

approaching hurricane all classes go virtual tomorrow

Steps to Writing Well

The first day of class, the teacher wears a sunshine smile and reviews the teaching methods, learning outcomes, weekly assignments, and grading procedures listed on the syllabus. Then she raises her voice that our assignments must meet her requirements. If the deadline for a paper is March 1, we can't put February 27 on the title page if we submit our assignment two days earlier. Otherwise, we lose five points. One student has the guts to ask whether he should never turn in his assignment before the deadline, but the teacher replies decisively that we must follow her guidelines closely. Time slides away week after week, and the teacher's sunshine smile looks like a cloudy moon since we keep losing points. When the semester ends, grievance forms swarm into the dean's office.

> *Well Done*
> written in red ink—
> does it mean
> a grade or
> barely read?

Open Enrollment

Sam walks into the conference room to enroll for the annual employees' insurance plan when a stout salesman in a dark red jacket comes up to market his life insurance. As Sam listens, thanks, and walks away, the red jacket blurts bluntly, "Buddy, if you died without life insurance, what would happen to your family?" Sam looks at the guy silently. "At least you need insurance to cover your funeral costs," the agent smirks. "You too," Sam returns a smirk and steps to a desk where a saleswoman greets him in a cotton-soft voice.

> Thanksgiving Day
> three weight loss emails
> in my Hotmail

New Page

After losing his job when the university suffered a drastic budget cut, Job has a handful of time to portion out to Muddy Waters, Howlin' Wolf, Charlie Parker, Monk, and Coltrane, who jazz up his days and blues his nights. He no longer needs to hurry to a morning class if getting up late. Instead, Job becomes a yardbird growing tomatoes, peppers, green beans, Swiss chard, and cucumbers. Only on a dull evening before watching an NBA game does he rest on the couch, pick up a blue ballpoint pen to scratch a lyric on a piece of paper, then crumble it into a ball to shoot a 3-pointer into the wastebasket— his poetry conservation for future mining.

> porch time
> on a napping man's lap
> *Catch-22*
> flipped at random
> by balmy breeze

Responses

Each weekday I drove past the corner of a campus street where two road signs named after Martin Luther King Jr. and Medgar Evers look like the open wings of a dragonfly canopied by a live oak, but I never stopped for a snapshot. During spring break, I went to campus to fetch some much-needed books. The university was like an empty cage. Thanks to its emptiness with no passing vehicles, I could stop by the signs to grab a shot. As I clicked, the signs fluttered their wings.

virtual commencement
after announcing each name
artificial cheers

Adjusting the Self

I have stopped eating meat; I eat more fruit: apple, banana, kiwi, navel, and blood orange. I also make peanut butter banana sandwiches and a fruit salad with pecans and raisins served with black tea.

> my friend in Alabama passes
> a cup of Da Hong Pao
> dissolves my sadness

The peanut butter banana sandwich was Elvis' favorite food. He liked crispy bacon in it. I got this recipe from an old friend in Alabama, a poet, violinist, and retired professor but not a singer. I like to toast two slices of wholegrain oatnut bread, spread peanut butter, and place sliced bananas on them like a row of dominoes pushed down.

> Memphis tour
> biting a burger
> at Beale Street
> where an Elvis fan
> swivels his hips

Though vitamin C supplement may work, I prefer fruit, sources of vitamin C, fiber, refreshment, and nutritional content that make me feel good each day and tint my life with juicy bites. Approaching retirement, I find myself writing more haiku, creating more photoku, and reading more haiku from books, magazines, and online haiku columns. Reading is a pleasure and gives me a break to decompress and reset my mind to creative thinking.

> naptime
> on the open book
> my folded glasses

Although haiku is as short as a bird's chirp, reading a fine haiku still requires a slowdown, a momentary stay, a snapshot in the mind's eye to gain an aesthetic taste. Like driving in the Smoky Mountains, an overlook or a roadside waterfall offers a moment to stop and grab shots before you move to the next scenic view. In a sense, haiku writing and reading, like a plate of fresh fruit salad, delights the mind.

prescription
for staying healthy...
one haiku a day

Goat

Wishing to offer more classes to help boost enrollment at the off-campus site, Dr. Kim, chair of the Education department, called Dr. Arrogante, a retiree in Arkansas hired as the site director in this rural Mississippi college. Her secretary answered the phone, saying Arrogante wasn't in yet. When Kim asked when she would be in, a gentle whisper—"Tell him I'll call him later"—tickled his ear. The secretary sounded like a Dictaphone. There was no callback. The next morning Kim called again, but no answer this time. He wondered, rocking in his squeaking chair. When enrollment plunged again at the off-campus site, the director waddled to Academic Affairs, whining she never received support from Education.

> hurricane gone
> the weathervane arrow
> points downward

Business Education

Professor Chow is suspicious of everything. You'd better pile up a flattering smile if you pass her in the hallway; otherwise, she says you show her a cold face. She likes to advise new hires, but they soon stay away from her burning sunlight. Chow also likes to check on her colleagues' office hours or peek into their offices as if she were a foreman keeping a sharp eye on everything. Now and then, her yell squeezes out of her office when students challenge their grades. Her business is no longer education.

> final exam week
> five grievance forms
> from graduating seniors

Healing

On that sunny morning, those fearless firefighters rushed to the Twin Towers of the World Trade Center to fight the devils from hell; they ran up and up and up, up into the crashing of the towers, up to be ashes, up to be phoenixes.

> Ground Zero
> stars and stripes
> flapping in wind

The Ferris Wheel of Life

After teaching three back-to-back algebra classes, Joe slumps into the swivel chair for a power nap, arms folded as a headrest and legs stretched out on an ottoman—a box of old books removed from the bookshelf.

> soft knock
> a student-athlete
> turns in his paper

Joe bites a banana sandwich, gulps a bottle of spring water, then hurries to the University Tenure and Promotion Committee meeting. The dossier review prolongs to 5 p.m., like a silent funeral service.

> driving home
> in the rearview mirror
> twilight disperses

The hour-long drive between home and work has been an irreplaceable distance in Joe's daily life that goes somewhere and nowhere, scenic one day in broad sunshine and slippery the other in howling rain.

> nightfall
> the moon over town
> a geisha's face

Notes

Two men scratch a chat over plates of oatmeal and sausages in Hotel Marlowe where they attend a literature conference. One asks the other where he's from. "Memphis." The word rolls like a coin across the table. (He's worked in that blues city for two decades.) Then he adds, like serving the shuttlecock underhand from below waist height, "I'm originally from South Korea." The receiver hits the shuttlecock, "Oh, I thought you were from Japan. I taught English there ten years ago."

> Tokyo tour
> asking for directions
> with a note in kanji

Mapping the Self

In August 1991, I left my job gracefully at a city college where I had taught for ten years and went to Southern Miss in Hattiesburg, Mississippi, to further my graduate studies. Attracted by her gentle voice, charming smile, beautiful figure, and southern warmth, I fell in love with Southern Miss. Each day I took a walk with her; each night I dreamed in her apartment. This was the only extramarital affair I've ever had. My wife remains blind to it, knowing I couldn't jump out of her hands no matter how many times I went out dancing with Southern Miss. After a five-year date with Southern Miss, I finished my academic performance on her dance floor with two diplomas, each like a memorandum of separation agreement. Yet, we both felt relieved when our affair ended with laughter like wind chimes.

> hop skip jump—
> double-dutch ropes somersault
> in memories

After bidding goodbye, not badbye, to Southern Miss, I didn't leave Mississippi. I relocated to the Delta, where I've lived close to the cotton fields for almost thirty years. This flatland offers me small but interesting views. Often on a quiet morning, I sit by the window, a camera in my hand, looking at the small yard tree with tiny white nuts dotting its slender branches. Blue jays, brown starlings, cardinals, mockingbirds, mourning doves, robins, sparrows, or rarely seen yellow warblers perch, preen, or leap on the tree. It's a small wonder how I've changed, unwittingly, from a migrating bird to a resident bird building a nest in the Delta, and how time has flown away so unnoticeably. Maybe it's because I've taken each day for granted.

> sunny Sunday
> a go-slow drive
> on blues highway

Mississippi sounds feminine. When the word is uttered, the vowel harmony chimes lovely and sexy. It's fertile soil for art and creative expression. That's why it's nurtured many great writers like William Faulkner, Tennessee Williams, Richard Wright, and Eudora Welty. In her notes about a memorable place, Welty said: "A place that ever was lived in is like a fire that never goes out. It flares up, it smolders for a time, it is fanned or smothered by circumstance, but its being is intact, forever fluttering within it, the result of some original ignition. Sometimes it gives out glory, sometimes its little light must be sought out to be seen, small and tender as a candle flame, but as certain." Mississippi is such a place that boosts and accommodates a feeling to write about it.

> weekend driving
> even the crunch of gravel
> sounds gleeful

Mississippi is rooted in the mind of everyone who's lived in or visited it and kept for it a fire that never goes out. This sense of place stimulates writing. Every writer has a sense of place in their heart, like warmth emanating from the fireplace; this sense can be a feeling or a quest to visit a place, settle down in a place, shape an identity, seek out a future, realize a dream, or write about a place; this sense has haunted my mind for modes of expression about life in the Delta, about mapping myself.

> alone time
> free from and
> for the self

Dream Song to the Comps

Night after night Plath blinks her sad eyes when Berryman sings his dream songs. Ashbery projects "the meaning as hard as" a stone cottage for me to break in when Joyce appears from nowhere to lead me into a maze where I wander like Mr. Bloom. Shoehorned in the heart of darkness, I wait for daybreak, not for Godot. My eyes are blurry. Words crawl like black ants or drift like floaters. Ford drops by to rescue me. He brags with flecks of spittle smearing onto Lawrence's cheeks: "I've found a good soldier," but the old man on the sea snorts his warning: "The sun rises. You need some shuteye." Rather, I follow Snyder to Cold Mountain to meet that monk, my steps on the riprap echoing the valley. In a heartbreak house on the wasteland, an invisible man is preparing a cocktail party for my reception. Eliot, who's conducting *Four Quartets*, offers his poetic advice: "The beginning is often the end." Pound cuts in, "No, the end should be the beginning." He greets me in Chinese and takes me to Williams, who signs his name on the back of a red wheelbarrow picture given to me. Getting a little tipsy, I bow my farewell and keep belching on my way to Howards End, murmuring "I have known them all already, known them all." O'Hara hurries up to me: "You need to see Kafka tomorrow in his country doctor's house." "Yeah, yeah, I know, I know." I wake up with Whitman's "Song of Myself" ringing in my ears.

> a fortune cookie slip
> pinched in fingers—
> patience is quality
> of a field dog
> hunting game

Dreamination

A strong shelf cloud, a rolling squall, the darkening sky. Popeye speeds into the darkness that swallows him at once into a symphony of booming thunder, cracking lightning, whistling storm, and drumbeating hail on top of his car. He presses hard on the gas pedal, and the car swerves, almost hitting the guardrail. When the storm finally abates into a serenade of drizzle, the car starts to crawl like a snail and its muffler toots like a squelching fart. Popeye strikes his fist on the steering wheel, yelling, "You junk guy, speed up!" But the car keeps crawling and tooting.

Finally, Popeye pulls up home. Standing listlessly on the doorsteps, he knocks on the door with an effort to raise his voice, "I'm back, honey."

"I'm coming." Olive Oyl's shrill voice answers the door first.

When the door finally opens, Popeye's eyes pop out. He shakes his head unbelievably and stares: Brutus, wearing a fool's cap, stands like a muscle wrestler in the doorway, grumbling, "Who are you?"

Before Popeye collects himself, Brutus kicks him up into the sky and shuts the door with a bang. After dropping onto the ground, Popeye takes out his iPhone and quacks like a duck for help, "Mao Zedong, tell me what I can do with that fool's cap."

A foreign, muffled voice from the glass casket, "Counterattack."

Hearing this, Popeye dumps spinach into his mouth and looks immediately like a kung fu master ready to strike Brutus' face into a poor man's pot pie. Suddenly, an old man shows up at the door, saying with his hands folded at the level of his heart as a mudra of greeting, "A settlement cannot be done with fists."

"Who's that wrinkle-faced man in a long robe?" Popeye makes a desperate uproar.

"He's Confucius, an educator I don't like." Mao sneers, frowns, and orders, "Flog that cur!"

The old, wrinkled man soon disappears while Popeye marches to the door. As Popeye stomps his feet into the room like a giant robot, Olive Oyl's feeble voice wafts from the bed, "Honey, this is Mr. Franz Kafka, my country doctor."

Olive Oyl sits in bed with a newborn mewling in her arms.

As soon as he sees the baby, Popeye pops his eyes again. "That son of bitch!" he grinds his corn-colored teeth. He feels like a man wearing a green hat, his fists squeezing shock and anger, and veins popping out of his arms. Scared by Popeye's volcanic fury, the doctor changes himself back into Brutus and runs away through the back door. Popeye screams and stomps, and the house shakes in a dismantling sound.

The dreamer's wife rolls up, stroking his shoulder and asking nervously, "Are you OK? You were screaming." "Wwwwhat?" The man mutters, turns his back on his wife, and snores.

on the round belly
of the laughing Buddha
a bright moon
empty shine
of silence

Before Separation

Home is where love groans like buzzing bees over a bed of sweet briar, where two rivers wiggle their graceful shapes of sinuosity into bodies, where two minds form a confluence to show a dynamic view of the bodyscape, where heart and soul overlap like building blocks until they shake and quake into pieces.

    broken heart
    flashing sparks from forging
    red hot metal

Angling

A red earthworm writhes on the hook. A catfish bites it, then flops, struggling in pain and panic to escape while the angler reels in the line. The world today is like a pond. Some nations are anglers while others are fish splashing on hooks.

> power outage
> news on Ukraine
> turns dark
> no moonshine
> this rainy night

IV

Driving on the Skyline through Shenandoah National Park

Every now and then, I stopped to grab some shots. At an overlook, a dead tree alone on the slope caught my attention. It stood against the impassive sky, its limbs broken, but its upright stiffness, sharp and stark, gave it the look of a scarecrow whose shabby clothes had been stripped by the wind.

    lakeside camp
    sunset crackles
    in the fire

Alone in Oahu

Waking late, I missed the group tour of the Polynesian Cultural Center. The lodge is as quiet as the leopard slug crawling on the bathroom floor. As I enjoy a paper bowl of crunchy frosted flakes, I fold out the map on the bed and use a yellow highlighter to mark the route of a bus ride that winds from Manoa to Waialua on the north shore and then to the scenic windward coast on the east of the island.

> cemetery tour—
> looking for Charlie Chan
> stone by stone

I hop onto a transit bus, sit by the window, and look out. Yet, the slow bus wobbles like a duck through residential areas and rocks me to shuteye. After a while, a soft scent tickles my nose and wakes me to look for the perfume wearer. Oh, the bus is riding through a pineapple farm. The mellow wind fills the bus. I close my eyes again to savor the scent as if it's relaxing piano music.

> daydream
> a Blackburn's Blue
> in and out

Morning Hike to the Makapuu Point in Oahu

We start our two-mile hike from the trailhead to the summit. As we climb, the warm ocean wind flaps wild past us.

> surging waves
> sunshine surfs
> on their crest

Now and then, the group stops to snap pictures: Koko Head, World War II bunkers, Rabbit Island, the deep blue ocean dazzling in the morning sun, the red-roofed lighthouse, white waves breaking on the black rocks.

> breaking waves
> each curl
> a shape of sunlight

Along the trail are the overgrown cacti, some blooming, some drying and drooping, some preserving human visits:

> halfway to the point
> tourists' names carved
> in cactus leaves

Mind Flash

During the month-long summer institute on East Asia in Oahu, I toured the island to satiate my wanderlust as much as I could, but upon returning to Mississippi, lingering before my eyes was nothing but a cat meowing in a bamboo grove outside the classroom. When wind arose, the bamboo clanked a melody like a muyu struck during temple chants. Sometimes I passed by to check on the cat and found him nestled there like a sage retiring from the hustle and bustle of society to the reclusive shade of the bamboo grove. I called him Sleeping Buddha, but he stretched his back legs and narrowed his eyes into a squint.

> still pond
> a Zen moment
> for koi

Mountain Views

At first, a red slit from the amniotic sac of the dark sky. Then the red baby gushes out, kicking legs and rolling like a mischievous giant panda. It crawls and looks around curiously. Soon it rolls up and stretches its arms to pluck chords of light so dazzling to the eye. Viewers, who have stood in awe for this grand moment or snapped shots, start to leave. A long line of cars winds down the mountain road to where we belong.

    screeching to stop
    at a sharp curve—
    a road-crossing elk

A Perfect Circle

At sunrise, I unfolded the map on the camp table to mark the road to the Blue Ridge Parkway. As the marker wound along, I spotted Mingo Falls! Only a few miles away. How did I miss that?

> view at an over-
> look—a passionflower
> in full blossom
>   for itself
>   for an overlook

I packed up and headed to the falls. The rugged trail meandered up along the creek. After I stood on the small wooden bridge, the sun sprinkled droplets of light over me.

> quiet dawn
> a bird's loud call
> here and there
>   sunbeams
>   through woods

In the summer of 2018, I revisited Mingo Falls on my way to Sapphire, North Carolina. The sun hid from rain, and the wooden bridge was no longer there.

> dark night
> a shooting star
> flashes out
>   sound sleep
>   without dream

Mid-October in the Smoky Mountains

We drive to see the fall foliage, but the cascades of color look as dull as a small town's faded murals. At an overlook, an old couple says the reason is that there hasn't been enough rain during the year. Then thunderstorms and lightning confine us to the resort for two days. We sit in balcony chairs, watch dark clouds somersaulting. When the storms slacken, we go to see the Harrisburg Covered Bridge. Each of its cut-out windows frames the same view: lines of rain and wisps of mist slanting in wind.

    black sky—
    hiding in a
    white wooden church

On the day of departure, the blue sky returns. We wind west on the Little River Gorge Road from Gatlinburg to Cades Cove. Along the way, we stop to shoot pictures of everything we can: watermill churning by a creek, fenced historic graveyard, replica of a pioneer log cabin. Above the muddy river, red, gold, yellow, and orange sparkle in morning sunshine.

    photo after photo
    the creek gurgles
    all night long

In the Mountains

The night rain pitapatting on our tent stops when the sun rises with a yawn and swings its long dreadlocks of light like a bluesman singing his heart out in a juke. We go hiking. On the trail to the waterfall, we clump on mud, laugh at the squelch made by our steps, and slog on until loud splashes fill our ears. We look up like pious pilgrims. The waterfall, a robed monk, stretches its arms.

> waking from nap
> on the cabin porch:
> a zebra longwing
> dances away
> from my dreamy eyes

Driving to Cades Cove

Golden leaves drift in midair, each a glide of sunlight dappling the road. Our car meanders in the woods to the gravesite of an Appalachian man. A tale says that he was killed for helping the Union army. By the wrought iron fence of the churchyard wrapped by silence, the man's small marble stone shines hard in the autumn sun, the inscription faded with the rub of time.

    spreading dusk
    the bloody sunset covered
    with a black sheet

Stay the Night

After the old T-Bird wheels around a bend, the GPS chimes "Welcome to Nevada." The sun bows out, and patches of clouds transform into black-cloaked ghosts roaming the darkening sky.

> boring drive
> a big yawn
> to tearful stars

When the car gasps over the hills, the city lights of Las Vegas dance like showgirls in the far distance. The road becomes a runway in the headlight, and the T-Bird gains speed to take off.

> empty hands
> his last greenback
> fed to the tiger slot

Road to Death Valley

After a boring drive through the barren land, I slide through the commercial zone of Pahrump, Nevada. Turning onto a narrow tar road, I jam on the brakes. Shocked by the sudden stop, my napping wife opens her eyes:

> noontime
> alone by the road
> a faded sign
> of no hitchhiking
> in the strong sun

As I roll down the window to snap a picture, the heat wave catches a chance to squeeze in, giving us a goofy grin. The car at once feels like a mini heat dome. I roll up the window, press the max AC button, and drag on.

> head shaking
> my wife asks why a sign
> deserves a photo
> take a break
> I whine to her

When we arrive at Mesquite Dunes, the blazing sun looks at us curiously and stamps red ink on us as if we are national park passports. Like chuckwallas, we scoot quickly into the car and run away in a string of farting noises.

New Year's Eve

After hiking the loop trail for two hours in the icy wind on Assateague Island, I see a gibbous moon hovering atop a dead pine. Its bare limbs stretch up as if wanting to hug her to dance me goodbye. I clap my cold hands and snap a shot. When I drive away, the lighthouse appears ahead. It winks. I pull off and wait patiently for a better snap. With the click of my camera, a soft blue glimmers on the horizon, like a promise.

> dissolving twilight
> a moonwalker's steps
> slide-switch

Second Looking

We walked into the Yatsu Rose Garden in Narashino before it was closed, surprised to find most roses had lost their bloom and looked like crepe paper. After looking at the faded roses of pink, white, blue, green, yellow, and purple, we paused by a red one named Dream, persistent in holding its color to offer us a moment of dreamination. On our way back to the hotel, the red twilight bloomed roses all over the western sky.

    falling leaf
    its shadow waits
    for the touch

Spicing

Wuhan, a river city called Furnace where "baniangyangdi" can spring off the tongue of a local. Three young men toss the b-phrase in their chat and laugh heartily by the mouth of the alley. Like a chef who needs to concoct his food, some locals go easy on coarse words to fire up their chat.

heat wave
a green fly buzzes
against the pane

Sound and Vision

Evening mist hovers along the canal as Benjamin Britten's "Suite No. 3" strolls away from a cello played in a riverside bar. Like lovers on a date, mist and solo waltz in the square, her white dress sliding gracefully with his black tuxedo. Then they pace hand in hand, their steps echoing on the cobblestone streets. When the bow lifts from the strings, they bid adieu. Mist drifts to the canal, and solo bows back to the cello. Both look back, loath to part. Somewhere the clock bell strikes. Lento solenne.

starry night
loneliness rolls out
its dark blue

In the Right Place at the Right Time

The sun hangs like a hotpot of boiling broth, so my wife and I take a break in the shade of a small broadleaf tree. A cicada nymph clings to a sprig. Nymphs usually emerge above ground at night to avoid predators. Why does this one molt at high noon? It looks like a small chunk of a mud dauber's nest. It's unfettering itself, but its slow molting is as tricky as if it's playing dead or stuck in its straitjacket. My wife urges me to go to the overlook first. After grabbing a couple of shots of her broad smile with shades of mountain ranges as the backdrop, I return to check on the nymph. It's now a green cicada clinging to its shell, soft green wings a chiffon blouse. As I hold up my camera, a loud chorus of cicadas rises overhead like cheers. These spirits, after sucking sap from tree roots for years underground, sing so gleefully and desirably for their short lifespan under the summer sun.

> camping night
> dream of our first kiss
> a lightning bug

In the Right Place at the Wrong Time

After the trail leads us to the gnarly and rocky creek side, our desire for waterfalls pops like a pricked balloon. Cherokee Falls trickles like silver gossamer. We turn around. At the fork where two signs point to Hemlock Falls and the parking lot, I persuade my wife we shouldn't give up Hemlock though it's not the right time to see waterfalls. We stumble down the knee-hurting meandering steps, disappointed again. Daniel Creek snakes through the lichen-covered boulders into a small fall like the Manneken Pis. No delightful aahs. We pant, leaning on the railing of a wooden bridge. We are desperate on our way back up, each step a big gasp of air. When we reach the mountaintop, red-faced with sticky sweat, we feel like shaky scarecrows wobbling to the parking lot.

    head-on
    too late to see the deer
    frozen in headlights

Homing

We rolled out of the mountains like dry tumbleweed on New Year's Day after wintering for two weeks in the Smokies where we honked our horns when driving through tunnels, explored frozen waterfalls, and stood on the windy overlooks to grab shots of bare views.

> cold night
> honking geese
> land in dream

We chose this day to be on wheels because eighteen-wheelers rarely trailed one after another like cars of a long freight train on I-40. The road was a magic flying carpet for cruising at a steady speed while sunrise followed us in the rearview mirror.

> home at last
> moon atop the pine
> a welcome lantern

Acknowledgments

The prose poems in this collection were written in the forms of haibun and tanka prose. They are linked forms. Prose and haiku or tanka are linked to complement each other through juxtaposition for a new sensibility, but they also stand independently with complete meanings of their own. They are also like short-shorts or nonfiction prose.

Many thanks to the editors of the acknowledged journals, who first published my work, and deep gratitude to Kim Davis, director, and Linda Parsons, poetry editor, of Madville Publishing.

Cantos: A Literary and Arts Journal: "Second Looking"
Cattails: "In the Drunk's Eye," "Road to Death Valley," "Stay the Night," "Steps to Writing Well"
Chrysanthemum: "In the Right Place at the Right Time," "Looking Out the Window"
Cloudbank: "In the Mountains"
Common Ground Review: "Morning Hike to the Makapuu Point in Oahu"
Contemporary Haibun Online: "A Perfect Circle," "A Stay Against Confusion," "A Way of Watching," "Driving on the Skyline through Shenandoah National Park," "Mid-October in the Smoky Mountains," "Moonplay," "Not in Vain," "The Existence of Time," "Then and Now," "Touch"
Drifting Sands: "A Stop in Port Gibson, Mississippi," "Dreamination," "Driving to Cades Cove," "Just Wondering," "Mind Flash," "Mountain Views," "Old Field Road Sign, Mount Locust, Mississippi," "Quiet Departure," "Right of Way," "Transference"
Failed Haiku: "Angling," "Business Education," "Missing," "Open Enrollment," "Responses," "Spicing"
Flash: "Goat," "In Another Country"
Frogpond: "Alone in Oahu"
Haibun Today: "New Year's Eve"
Haiku Page: "Adjusting the Self" (originally titled "Introduction")
Intégrité: "The River of God"
New World Writing Quarterly: "Sightseeing"

Open: Journal of Arts & Letters: "Attachment," "Dream Song to the Comps"
Poetry East: "Killing Time"
Ribbons: "New Page"
2River: "Memory of Mom's Cat"
San Pedro River Review: "A Delta Weekend"
The Stillwater Review: "Sound and Vision"
Under the Basho: "Homework," "Notes"
Valley Voices: "Goodbye," "Mapping the Self," "River," "A Sense of Place," "Where Are You From?"

About the Author

Jianqing Zheng is the author of *The Dog Years of Reeducation*, *A Way of Looking*, and five poetry chapbooks and e-chapbooks; editor of seven scholarly books, including *Conversations with Dana Gioia* and *Sonia Sanchez's Poetic Spirit through Haiku*; and coeditor of four scholarly books, including *Dana Gioia: Poet & Critic*. He received the 2019 Gerald Cable Book Prize, 2001 Slapering Hol Press Chapbook Award, and three poetry fellowships from the Mississippi Arts Commission, among other awards and honors. He is professor of English at Mississippi Valley State University, where he serves as editor of the *Journal of Ethnic American Literature* and *Valley Voices*. His poems have appeared in numerous magazines, including *Another Chicago Magazine*, *Birmingham Poetry Review*, *Louisiana Literature*, *Mississippi Review*, and *Spillway*.